REPAIR YOUR CREDIT LIKE THE PROS!

Learn Proven Tactics And Strategies

To Beat The Credit Agencies And Rebuild

Your Credit

Danny Cole

Repair Your Credit Like The Pros

Learn Proven Tactics And Strategies To Beat The Credit Agencies and Rebuild Your Credit

Publication Date 2018

Published By: Cole-Han Publishing

UpdateCreditRepair.com

ISBN 978-0-578-20106-1

Library of Congress Number: 2018930572

Table Of Contents

Introduction

I wrote this book for those who are tired of getting turned down for loans and credit cards. Those who are tired of paying high interest rates. This book is for real people, like you and me, looking for real solutions to their credit problems. This book contains proven tactics and strategies on how to beat the credit agencies, repair your credit, and improve your credit score.

Credit is something that most people have heard about, but few people truly understand. A good credit score is important for more reasons than just obtaining new credit. These days, it can factor into everything from landing a new job to getting the best deal on your insurance, car, and home. As both someone who owns a credit repair business and someone who has been in the sales industry for 20 years, I felt it was my duty to write this book on credit repair for everyone who has ever had credit problems or questions.

The good news is no credit score lasts forever. Your score can go up or down depending on how you manage your credit. Your goal with this guide is to take action that will improve your credit lifestyle. No matter what mistakes you have make in the past, no matter what challenges you face with your finances today, or even what you have been told about your credit, you can repair and rebuild your credit and begin to make a positive impact in yours and your family's future today. The most valuable life changing information about credit is inside this book.

I have sold everything from cars and real estate, to life insurance, and as you can imagine, I have seen to many good hearted, honest, hardworking people get turned down for something they absolutely needed or wanted. And over my years in the sales industry I've learned two undeniable truths; Cash may be king, but credit is power, AND, Bad credit happens to good people.

Think about it for a moment, without credit you cannot buy a house, a car, rent an apartment, get certain jobs, or basically anything now. Credit is vital to you living a normal life. It is vital if you want to purchase a vehicle with no money down. It is vital if you do not want to pay a high interest rate. It is vital if you do not want to over pay for something you are financing. It is vital if you want to save money for the future. And most importantly, it is vital for you and your family's overall wellbeing and financial stability.

But, unfortunately there are millions of people all around this country who are currently experiencing or have suffered troubles with bad credit in the past. So, if you have bad credit, do not worry, you are not alone. Plus, feel good knowing you are reading this book right now which means you are aware of the importance of having good credit and you are one step closer to actually achieving a good credit rating and improving your overall quality of life.

Even though your credit rating may seem like an intangible asset, it is one of the most valuable and important assets that you have. Without a good credit rating your financial, occupational, personal, and family goals are at risk of being severely limited. You see, in order to even obtain the privilege of using a credit card, your credit rating is checked.

If a company determines your credit to be unsatisfactory, you will be denied a credit card. From the moment you are denied, your quality of living is limited. If you can't get something as simple as a credit card, you can't rent a car, order tickets to a show, or open a checking account. Because your credit rating was determined to be unsatisfactory, most companies will not let you use their money.

Today, more than ever, businesses perform routine background checks during the hiring process. For instance, if there are two equally qualified applicants, you and someone else, for the same position, your potential employer could compare the credit reports of the both of you and give the position to the applicant with a better credit rating. This may not seem fair, but they are judging their decision based on what they see as reliable, trust worthy, and responsible.

Since maintaining a good credit rating is important in today's society, a poor credit rating can have a negative snowball effect toward your goals. Good, strong credit allows you to live with financial security and enables you to purchase items without depleting your life savings.

Repairing your credit can seem like a monumental task; however, it can also be as easy as following the process outlined in this book and implementing the tactics and strategies, or even easier, by enrolling for credit repair with my company, Update Credit Repair LLC (updatecreditrepair.com). Your decision to repair your credit rating will benefit you for the rest of your life. The more time you invest now toward strengthening your credit rating, the better your quality of life will be. And as with everything else in life, the sooner you get started the sooner you will see results. Don't wait until it is too late.

This guide is intended to support and help individuals and families find the answers to the most commonly asked questions on credit repair and give them proven strategies and tactics to legally and quickly repair and rebuild their credit.

After reading our guide, you will have the basic

knowledge to getting out of debt, as well as information that will guide you to resources that will help you repair your credit, get loans, and so forth. This is a must read guide for anyone that has bad credit, no credit, or trying to establish credit.

What Is Your Credit Score

Your credit score is an overall view of your borrowing and payment history over the past 7 to 10 years. In a nutshell, your 3-digit credit score tells lenders how likely you are to repay loans. Or, your credit worthiness. Lenders use your score to determine your eligibility for loans, lines of credit, credit cards, etc.

The lower your score is the lower your chances are of getting a loan, credit card, apartment, insurance, home, car, etc. The higher your score is the more opportunities you will have available to you to buy a new car, get a home mortgage loan, or a major credit card, from any source, with low interest rates. Generally speaking, the higher the score the better. Your credit score plays a significant role in the loan approval process.

Credit reports can also be used by employers for employment purposes, by insurance companies to determine rates, by landlords to determine if they will rent to you, and several other situations. In fact, with today's society becoming more and more business oriented, establishing and maintaining good credit is vital if you plan to do any of the following:

1. Apply for employment
2. Rent an apartment
3. Open a bank account
4. Setup an account with public service or the telephone company
5. Get a cell phone
6. Save for the future
7. Finance a vehicle
8. Finance a home

It used to be that establishing good credit was important only if you planned to buy a home or a car, but not anymore. The simplest necessities such as turning on your utilities require good credit, unless you want to overpay or get a co-signer.

What Determines Your Credit Score

There are 5 main factors that determine your credit score. I will list them in order from most heavily weighed to least.

Payment History

This makes up for 35% of your score. Credit Reporting Agencies (CRAs) want to see how you have paid off past loans, and if you paid them on time. If your credit is good, one or two late payments may not affect the overall picture. 30 days late, is less damaging than being 60 or 90 days late. Needless to say, late is late. Pay your bills on time because this is the biggest determining factor.

Debt To Credit Ratio

Your debt to credit ratio is how much debt you have compared to the available credit you have. This makes up a whopping 30% of your credit score. How many cards you have does not weigh as heavily as how much you owe. If your cards are maxed out, your score will drop, and you will be considered a high risk. Having a high credit limit and not using it shows responsibility and helps your score. You want to have your debt to credit ration at 30% or less. If you are more than 30% then it will negatively affect your score.

Length Of Credit History

15% of your credit score is based upon how long you have had credit for. With this being said, if you have one of earliest, or even better, your very first credit card, do not cancel it. Because by canceling it you will only lower your credit score. If you are wanting to cut down on having so many open credit card accounts, choose one that is newer. By doing this you still maintain your length of credit history which helps your credit score.

Types Of Credit

10% of your credit score is based upon the types of credit you have. The CRAs like to see a healthy mix such as; mortgage, car, credit card, retail accounts, secured, unsecured, and revolving.

New Credit

10% of your score is from credit inquires, credit applications and new accounts. It doesn't look good to apply for 5 credit cards at once. It looks like you are desperate for credit and will negatively affect your score.

But, keep in mind, if you are car shopping or house shopping the CRAs will not weigh the inquires the same. Typically, if you purchase a vehicle within 14 days of having your credit ran numerous times it will only count as 1 inquiry. You have 45 days for a home. After that, when you pull your credit again, it will be another hard pull.

Get Your Credit Reports

Now that you understand how your credit score is determined and why you need good credit, the next question is, how do you get started repairing your credit? You start by requesting a copy of your credit reports. You should order copies of all three of your credit reports from the three major reporting bureaus; Equifax, Transunion, and Experian.

You are entitled by Federal Law to receive a free annual credit report once a year. But, it can be a little confusing obtaining your credit report with so many companies promising that they are the best resource.

Some companies offer reports, but no scores while others offer scores, but no reports. Some even use different scoring models. There are FICO, Vantage, CE, etc. And to make it even more confusing there are different versions of each model.

FICO

FICO, headquartered in San Jose, California was founded by Bill Fair and Earl Isaac in 1956. There are 49 different versions of your score that FICO determines based upon your credit history and it sends them to inquiring lenders. Different lenders will receive different scores. So, your FICO score for your auto loan will be slightly different than that of your mortgage loan. Your FICO score for your insurance will be slightly different than that of your department store, etc.

Your FICO score is the most important score that you want to have access to. It is considered the most reliable resource due to it having the best track record. FICO scores are also the most widely used scores by lenders to determine if you will be approved or denied for your major purchases.

Your FICO score will range anywhere from 300 to 850. According to Experian, a credit score of 579 and lower is considered poor. A credit score between 580-669 is fair. 670-739 is considered a good. 749-

799 is very good, and a credit score above 800 is considered excellent. 640 is where you begin to see the lower interest rates begin to happen.

Here is the breakdown:

800+	1,485 to 1
720-799	659 to 1
680-719	112 to 1
620-679	47 to 1
Below 620	15 to 1

What this means is, for every 15 consumers with credit scores below 620 that lenders lend money to, 1 out of the 15 will default by 90 days.

Which in turn means, for the lender to make money they must charge more interest to those with lower scores to offset the losses of the 1 who defaulted.

How To Get Your Credit Reports For FREE

Obtaining credit reports and credit scores can cost money. You can easily spend hundreds of dollars on them if you are frequently ordering them throughout your credit repair process. (If you sign up at UpdateCreditRepair.com for credit restoration, you will receive free monitoring of your credit scores and will also receive notices when your score increases.) So, who, or where, is the best resource to obtain your scores from. I have compiled a list of 5 sources you could choose from.

Credit Karma – creditkarma.com offers free scores and reports. You will receive 2 scores and 2 reports from TransUnion and Equifax at no cost.

Credit Check Total – creditchecktotal.com is owned by Experian and will provide all 3 credit scores and reports. You will have to pay $1 to start your 7-day trial to get them, but all you have to do is cancel after you get the copies of your reports and scores.

Annual Credit Report – annualcreditreport.com gives you all 3 credit reports for free, but no scores. This is the only way to get a no strings attached copy of all 3 credit reports.

My FICO – myfico.com is a little expensive, but it will provide all 3 scores and reports for you. Unless, sign up for a subscription.

Free Score 360 – freescore360.com is another site that will give you all 3 scores and reports, but you will have to sign up for the 7-day trial. If you cancel before the 7 days are up then you will only be charged $1, just like Credit Check Total.

And even if you have already received a free credit report for the current year you may still obtain a second report. How? Good Question. If you were denied credit for any reason you may use that letter of credit denial to get the second report.

All you have to do is send in a copy of that denial letter within 60 days of its receipt with your written request. Be sure to include a copy of your state issued ID, proof of your address and your last known addresses for the past 5 years. It is also very important to include a copy of your social security card for ID verification.

Who Are The Credit Agencies

The "Big 3" credit bureaus are Equifax, TransUnion, and Experian. They are NOT government agencies. And make no mistake about it, these are for-profit privately-owned billion-dollar companies. These credit bureaus and the creditors have one thing in common, and that is, the worse your credit is the more money they make.

The Credit Agencies, Credit Bureaus, or the Credit Reporting Agencies, which ever name you wish to call them by, collect information from your existing credit accounts as well as your payment history from a variety of institutions. Some of these institutions are mortgage companies, credit card companies, banks, telephone companies, utility companies, etc., then they sell it right back to them after they determine your credit worthiness by compiling your information compared to everyone else's information.

You see, for instance, when credit card companies pay a large amount of money for lists of consumers for whom they will target with their cards, they do not want consumers that have great credit on those lists. Why? Because they know that consumers with great credit will qualify for better interest rates and not need to be solicited with promotional offers. Also, those with great credit will choose the credit card company they want to do business with, and not get chosen by them.

So, when the credit bureaus send these lists to their customers (credit card companies and anyone else purchasing them) they do not verify the accuracy and validity of them. The more errors the better. They make more money on consumers with lower credit scores.

Equifax

Equifax is the oldest and largest credit bureau around today. They were founded in 1899 in Atlanta, Ga. as a retail credit company by two brothers, Cator and Guy Woolford. The company is still based in Atlanta, Ga. today. Equifax grew extremely fast from the day it was founded and by the late 1960's it had already grew to one of the largest credit bureaus with close to 300 locations.

In fact, they became so large that they drew the attention of our federal government. And so, in 1971, the US Congress enacted the Fair Credit Reporting Act to regulate the information that the credit bureaus could buy and sell. The Fair Credit Reporting Act was the first of several Acts put in place by our government to protect the consumer.

Between October 2012 to September 2017 Equifax had the most complaints and disputes relating to inaccurate, incomplete, and outdated information. The number was over 57,000 consumer complaints. Equifax operates in 14 different countries and its annual revenue is 3.1 Billion dollars.

TransUnion

TransUnion is the smallest of the "Big 3" credit bureaus but was the second of the "Big 3" to come along. After starting out as a holding company for the Union Tank Car Company in 1968, they soon acquired the Credit Bureau of Cook County one short year later propelling them into the credit business.

TransUnion began to buy up all the credit bureaus it could in major cities and still does to this day. They grew to over 250 offices all across the U.S. as well as in 24 other countries.

TransUnion was purchased by Goldman Sachs Capital Partners and Advent International in 2010. TransUnion is based in Chicago, IL with offices in 25 countries and its annual revenue is 1.7 Billion dollars.

Experian

Experian is the last of the "Big 3" to enter the scene. They were founded in 1980 in England as CNN, Commercial Credit Nottingham. In 1996 they expanded into the U.S. by acquiring TRW Information Systems and Services Inc. and sold to two Boston private equity firms: Bain Capital and Thomas H. Lee Partners.

Experian is based in Dublin, Ireland and operates in 37 countries. Its annual revenue is 4.6 Billion dollars.

FTC

Credit Bureaus are monitored by the Federal Trade Commission (FTC) beneath the requirements of the Federal Fair Credit Reporting Act (FCRA) and follows up with the State Laws. If you have credit files with inconsistencies the Fair Credit Reporting Act protects you in the sense that it requires the credit bureaus to delete or make the information obsolete on your credit file. Otherwise you can file a lawsuit and win a maximum of $1,000.

This protects you if you are a victim of Identity Theft, false accusations, or inaccurate items and accounts made against you. The Credit Bureaus are required by the laws to list accuracies on credit files by gathering the appropriate information against you or on your behalf.

The laws protect you in the sense that it regulates the credit bureaus by only allowing them to list negative reports against you for a limited time. The laws also regulate who can see your credit files. If you are applying for a loan, license, public assistance, insurance, landlords, and courts can request your credit files without your consent.

The FTC conducted a study between 2002 and 2014 that determined about 40 million people across the United States had at least one error on one of their major credit reports. These errors affected their scores and cost the consumers thousands of dollars in higher interest rates on loans and other fees based on credit history.

LexisNexis

LexisNexis was founded in 1997 and is headquartered in Alpharetta, Ga. It is the company known for collecting and selling information insurers use to assess risk and streamline the underwriting process in 99% of all U.S. insurance claims and more than 90% of all homeowner claims.

The company collects information that commercial organizations, government agencies, and nonprofits use to profile individuals, businesses, and assets with data and analytic products.

LexisNexis has a ton of information on you and they are the company that the credit bureaus use to collect information on you for bankruptcies and other public records.

So, You Have A Copy Of Your Credit Report, Now What

Just because you have a copy of your credit report and can read it, doesn't help you understand it any better. And understanding what is on there and what the reports are saying is what is going to help you repair your credit.

(Here are 2 links, that you will need to copy and paste into your browser, that are examples of credit reports and how to understand them.)
http://www.experian.com/credit_report_basics/pdf/samplecreditreport.pdf
https://www.myfico.com/products/ficoone/sample/creditreport/sample_summary.aspx

Spend some time and effort studying over the credit reports and you will begin to understand them better. Once you receive each report you want to analyze every bit of information on it. Now, some reports are easier to read than others, but it is crucial that you take your time and go over every single line of information. You want to check for accuracy.

Remember, no one is going to contact you and inform you if some of your information is wrong on your credit report and negatively affecting your credit rating. It us up to you to do your due diligence and make sure all the information provided on them is correct. Your money and your family's financial future depends on it.

If any of your information is incorrect then report back to the Credit Reporting Agencies (CPAs) immediately. The bureaus are required by law to investigate any and all inaccuracies reported. The creditor has 30 days from date of notice to send out a response or the inaccurate information on the credit history has to be deleted.

What Can Legally Be Disputed On My Credit Report

After you have requested your credit reports, you can

move onto the next step. If you have any charges on your credit report that appears suspicious be sure to contact the three credit bureaus immediately, disputing the charges. If you have any information that is incorrect or unverifiable, then dispute those claims also.

The claims against your report affect you, so you have the right to file a claim with the Fair Crediting Reporting Act (FCRA). In 1971, the US Congress passed a law to protect us, the consumer, against claims filed on our credit report that do not belong to us. Take advantage of this law. Understanding the steps to credit repair is essential to get on the road to building credit.

Did you know that there are more than 26 parts of an account that all must be reported 100% complete, accurate, and verifiable? If any of these 26 parts are inaccurate, unverifiable, misleading, obsolete, or even questionable, then you have the right to dispute the account. This is why it is crucial that you go through your reports with a fine-tooth comb and search for anything that can be disputed. Many people don't realize that the credit bureaus are required to investigate your claims within 30 days and respond.

3 Important Areas To Examine On Your Credit Report

There will be 3 main areas for you to pay special attention to on your credit report. These areas are:

Personal Profile – This area covers your name, SSN, date of birth, current and past addresses, employers and aliases. Check for spelling and validity of all the information provided. You will probably want to dispute any aliases you do not want to have on your credit report. If there are any previous addresses you do not want on your report, or if they are misspelled, then dispute those as well. Take your time and thoroughly go through everything.

Account History – This area will break down your accounts and the information about them. It will provide the creditor's name, account number, date opened, monthly payment, high balance, late payments and balance owed. Pay close attention to the information provided. You will often find mistakes here. Often this section is color coded to make it easier to see your derogatory items.

Public Records – This area is extremely important to pay attention to. This area has the ability to significantly and singled handedly ruin your credit. In this area information such; bankruptcies, tax liens, judgements, and all others public records will be recorded. Bankruptcies can stay on your credit report for 10 years or more. Judgements can stay on your credit for 10 years or more. And liens can stay on your reports indefinitely. So, again, pay close attention to every detail and make sure that everything is 100% correct.

Other Areas To Check For Accuracy

Then there are several other mistakes that are commonly made. Just some of those are:

- Account paid off but still shows having a balance
- Same debt appearing more than once
- Identity theft. Make sure all the accounts were opened by you.
- Debt still showing after time of expiration. Most are seven years while bankruptcies are for 10 years.
- Mistaken Identity
- Inquires Section
- Wrong date of last activity showing
- Wrong balance listed
- Wrong credit limit amount listed
- Wrong charge-off date listed
- Wrong status listed
- Wrong original credit information listed
- Wrong amount listed

Understanding The Facts

Credit Repair is very effective, but results will vary greatly. They will vary based upon the knowledge you have about the process and the way in which you dispute. If you send in the same generic letter, written the same way, for the same dispute, then you will significantly decrease your chances of having the item you are disputing removed from your credit report.

You see, the large majority of the dispute letters getting sent to the bureaus are being scanned by a computer system. Two to be exact. If they get kicked out of the two computer systems, then they will be looked at by a live body. So, until then, no one will see or read your letter, no matter how sad and compelling it may be. These automated systems have made it easier and faster for the bureaus to read each letter and void it at every chance they can get.

Should You Dispute Everything At Once

This is a question that often gets asked. And there are varying opinions. So, let me tell you a little about the process so you can understand the answer I give.

Like I briefly mentioned earlier, there are two automated computer systems your dispute goes to. First, OCR and then e-OSCAR.

OCR or Optical Character Recognition is the first automated computer system that the bureaus have in place to determine if the dispute is legitimate or what they call frivolous. OCR not only attempts to determine if the dispute is legitimate or frivolous, but also stores these dispute in a detailed database.

It will store information from the dispute such as; name, spelling, color of font, paper size, font, so it will recognize if you have used the same template or dispute before. This is why you will have varying success with disputing if you do not have knowledge of the system. If OCR detects the same account with the same dispute letter it will mark it as frivolous and will not even investigate the dispute. Which is not good.

E-OSCAR or Online Solution For Complete and

Accurate Reporting is the web based automated dispute system used by the "Big 3" credit bureaus. This computer system is where the credit bureaus input disputes and those disputes are then delivered to the Data Furnisher or creditor who the dispute is for.

It is similar as OCR in the fact that the bureaus use it to quicken the process and eliminate human error. The system reads your dispute letter and automatically assigns a 2-digit code to it specifying what type of dispute it is; account was not late, not your account, account is paid in full, etc.

Then the code and the account are sent to the creditor and the creditor does one of 3 things; they validate that the account is accurate, delete the account due to inaccuracy, or do not respond at all, in which case it will be deleted in 30 days.

How To Successfully Dispute

The 7 most successful methods in disputing items

from your credit reports are listed below. These are some of the easiest and most proven tactics that will get items deleted from your credit report. Use these combined with the dispute letters found later in this book.

Have Spelling Errors - By having spelling errors, you have a greater chance of the dispute getting kicked out of the computer system and into the hands of a live person who will delete the dispute.

Do Not Use The Same Template Or Format – Change the format in which you write the dispute letters. If you use the same format or template OCR will already have it stored form the first dispute letter and flag it as frivolous.

Use Different Size Pape – Use different size paper for each dispute. Use notebook paper for one, then legal **r** paper for another, etc. The goal is not to get flagged by the computer system.

Use Pen, Pencil, Marker, and Crayon – Use an array of writing utensils. If your first letter to the bureau was in pen, make the second one in pencil. If it was in pen, make the next one a magic marker. Keep it different.

Use Different Size Font – If you are going to type your dispute letters then use different size font throughout your letter. You do not want the computer system to recognize the letters you are sending, and you do want the system to kick it out due to not understanding the format so that a live person gets your letter in their hands.

Use Heavier Paper – Use card paper or any paper that is heavier than the norm. The reason for that the dispute letter cannot be fed into the system and will get put into the hands of a live person.

Do Not Make It Look Professional – You do not want to make it look professional. Misspell words. Enter words or sentences that do not make sense. By doing this you increase your chances of the dispute letter not being read by the computer systems.

*** And be sure to include a sentence on the credit bureau dispute letter that states your request to a response to your dispute letter by mail. Because then by law they are required to respond by mail to your dispute letter.***

So, to answer the earlier question, should you dispute everything all at once? Yes. Dispute it all at once because it will be going to the OCR and e-OSCAR systems anyway. You want them to all get kicked out of the system and into the hands of a live person and if they have too much going on they will more than likely just delete the items instead of researching and verifying each and every one of them.

What Does It Mean To Have Good Credit? Who Cares?

Having good credit is everything. It tells businesses and people, and especially those people in business who are in the position of approving or denying your loan, if you adhere to your promises. If you are stable. If you follow through on your financial obligations. And if you do, then you most likely are a good and reliable person. You may be worth giving a chance at that once in a lifetime job, or beautiful residence in that perfect community, etc.

"Businesses look into your credit report and determine, by your ability to pay and follow through on your promises, what kind of person you are."

Who Can I Turn To For Help?

If you have been declined for a credit card, a loan, an apartment, or anything else, then it is time to get started on rebuilding or establishing your credit. But, who do you turn to for help? With an abundance of resources and companies available today that claim they can do this for you it can get overwhelming. Everywhere you turn you see someone willing to "Help Fix Your Credit."

Some are better than others and some less expensive than others. But, who can you trust? Who will really get the results they promise? Who will not over charge you? Do you pay more in hopes that one will be better because they are more expensive? Or, do you go with the most inexpensive option hoping they are just wanting to help?

With so many companies out there, it is hard to go through them all, but I can tell you, I have had clients tell me that they have worked with companies for a two years and their score has gone up only a few dozen points and only about half of their derogatory items had been removed.

Some companies do this because the longer you stay with them they more money they make. In my opinion, this is unsatisfactory. Then I recently had a person email me and tell me that someone told them they would "start" her process (with only 3 derogatory times) for $3,500. Start the process for $3,500! I don't know about you, but this is outrageous.

Let me tell you a little about me and why I do what I

do. As you already know, my name is Danny Cole and I have been in the sales industry for 20 years. I have sold everything from cars, real estate, life insurance, high-end furniture and everything in between. I love sales and I love helping people. There is not greater feeling in the world than helping someone get something they really desire.

But unfortunately, over my span of 20 years in sales I have seen too many good people get turned down for financing for something they either needed or wanted, due to uneducated mistakes made in their past. And to be honest, it sucked. I hated seeing it. I hated seeing the look of defeat in their eyes and the sad look on their face knowing they had to explain to their loved ones that they couldn't get what they so eagerly and happily came in the store for.

Why did I hate it? Because I know what it is like to have bad credit affect your life. You see, I grew up poor. And being the oldest of 6 kids, growing up on government assistance (food stamps) and primarily shopping at thrift stores for your school clothes, I know what it is like to struggle. I know what it is like to not have good credit and the consequences of it. Having to watch my parents ask others for help by co-signing or paying for what we needed and us paying them back. I know what it is like to live paycheck to paycheck, eating chicken pot pies several times a week because they were cheap and filling. (By the way, I never want to eat chicken potpies again)

Growing up poor, no one taught me about credit and how to build it, and I don't know about you but, school sure enough didn't teach me. But, for me everything happens for a reason. There are no coincidences in life. The past I experienced combined with the knowledge I have gained over my sales career and owning my credit repair business, has empowered me. It has empowered me with the knowledge of how to beat the credit agencies, attain and maintain good credit, and I want to empower others with the same power. My goal is to help 100,000 individuals and families achieve financial stability and financial freedom in their lives.

And starting a credit repair business was my way of achieving this goal. While I was in the process of starting my own credit repair business and attaining my certifications I continuously came across a company that was doing the same thing I wanted to do, but even more than I had planned. Financial Education Services (FES).

Financial Education Services was established in 2004 and is A+ rated with the Better Business Bureau. But, not only do they provide credit restoration, but they also provide 13 other programs. Yes, you read that correctly, 13 other programs, including; Credit Builder, Credit Attorney, Smart Credit, Fes Debt Zero, LifeLock, Financial Lockbox, Life Insurance, MyCare Plan, YFL Family Mint, Rx Discount Card, FES Travel, Health Insurance, and Discount Shopping. Copy and paste the link www.fesprotectionplan.com to learn more about the programs offered.

So, I started my company Update Credit Repair LLC. under Financial Education Services, and together we provide the best service in the credit repair industry. We have gotten bankruptcies, liens, late pays, evictions, slow pays, foreclosures, inquires, incorrect SSN's, incorrect date of birth, incorrect place of employment, incorrect address, etc., removed from credit reports. Because of this, we have helped good people, just like you, get the house, car, job, and credit they deserve, and help them save a ton of money in the process. Sounds good right?

And we handle the entire disputing process for you. No stress of having to research who, what and where to send the dispute letters. No having to keep up with when you sent the letters in and when to respond back with the follow up letters. No stress, no worries. We keep it simple.

You can even check your report credit everyday if you like, without effecting your credit score. If you are interested in working with a company that puts you first and does not cost an arm and a leg, then checkout my website, www.UpdateCreditRepair.com.

We not only help others take back control of their lives by taking control of their credit and finances, but we also provide an opportunity for you to become an agent, like myself, and help others do the same and make money in the process.

If becoming a credit repair agent, an entrepreneur, getting tax write offs, working from home, and making money while helping others, all for less than $300, interest you, then, checkout www.welcometofinancialfreedom.com or www.financialeducationservices.com/Opportunity.asp x?rid=dcole6 for more info. Watch the video and personally email me at.

www.UpdateCreditRepair@gmail.com or signup at www.UpdateCreditRepair.com

(P.S. Did I mention, you could get all the services mentioned above as an agent for free)

If you do not partner with my company to get your credit restored or another reputable company, make sure you do it yourself. My ultimate desire is for you to restore your credit and become financially free for you and for your family. If you see that there are claims against you it is your responsibility to handle them. There is no magical credit ferry that will take care of it for you. You must take action right away because the longer you wait the more difficult it is.

Many people around the world are filing bankruptcy, consulting with debt management programs, counselors, and other resources to find a solution to get out of debt. And it is easy to see why. With the economy in the shape it's in and business downsizing and people losing their jobs, it's no wonder. It's easier for your scores to drop like a rock from one late payment than it is for it to increase from making a payment.

Don't let bad credit ruin your life. We all have difficulties and sometimes we can't avoid obstacles that get in our way. Bad credit can lead to judgments against us, lawsuits, foreclosures, repossessions and so on. When we have bad credit, we are subject to becoming homeless, broke, hungry and then some. The key then to success is to find a solution that works best for you. If you are working or even on Welfare or Disability it is still possible to reestablish your credit.

Debt Relief

Credit repair is not always easy, but there are solutions available to help you restore your credit and at the same time, get out of debt. Now, prepare yourself to deal with paperwork and phone time once you are ready to repair your credit. But, trust me, it will be worth it.

Take Responsibility - Let's face it, having debt and bad credit is a stressful situation. There are many people all over the world on medication due to all the stress that the situation causes. And if affects everyone. I have seen people who make $20k a month get turned down on a $2k loan. (Yes, you read that right. I have seen people get turned down for a 2k loan who make $20k a month.)

You may be a good person, you may even be the most considerate and compassionate person alive; however, if your credit report shows a late payment or even worse, no payment on an account at all, your entire being could be perceived as not reliable, unstable and untrustworthy.

But in most cases, with patience and persistence, you can find a way out of debt and restore your credit. We will discuss some options you may have available to you to get out of your debt and get back on track with your credit.

There are many steps we can take to eliminating debt. And the best solution for getting out of debt is taking responsibility of your situation. Once you accept responsibility, you can overcome the situation. Taking responsibility puts you in the driver seat and gives you power.

Millions of people around the world, at one time or another, have had some type of financial change that has affected them negatively, i.e. a loss in the family, loss of a job, or medically. Therefore, you are not alone and there are many others that are aware of this fact.

The most important step to repairing credit is staying up to date on your bills. If you feel that you can't make a payment it is wise to make contact with the creditor letting them know there will be a delay on payment. Creditors often prefer that you call them to negotiate a payment plan and sometimes creditors will even lower your monthly payments, or even your bill.

Insurance Options - Now let's take a look at some of the options you may have available to you. If you are in debt and own a home, you probably have insurance coverage. If so, you might be able to take an advance payment against your insurance policy. Call your insurance agent and find out if you can.

Also, Life Insurance Coverage may offer a payback solution after you have paid in on the plan for a length of time. Call your life insurance agent and find out if you do. In either case, if you are able to get a lump sum be sure to be responsible and pay off your debts rather than spending your money freely.

If you are suffering debt problems related to injuries or even suffer a terminal illness some policies will make payments on your mortgage until you are back on your feet again. If you are off work due to being unemployed, as no result of your own, then you may be qualified on your insurance policy for a type of coverage that makes your payments for you until you are back at work.

Refinance Options - If you don't have insurance coverage, or you have insurance coverage that doesn't offer these options, you may want to check with your lender or local credit union to find out if there is a refinance loan available to you that offers lower monthly installments and lower interest rates.

What about car payments? Are you paying a fortune on your car each month? If so, you may be able to refinance your car. I would check with your local credit union because they usually have the best rates. If you can lower your car payments, then you can use the extra money to pay off your debts or put money in savings.

Take A Small Loan Out – Going to your local bank that you are a part of, or my preference, a credit union, and taking out a small loan is a great option of getting out of debt quicker and raising your credit score.

If you do get into another loan you want to make sure that you are not paying more than you already are. If you decide to take out a refinance loan, make sure that you are aware of the upfront fees that often are included in mortgage loans.

Pay off the credit card debt with the small loan you take out. Do not spend it. You will almost instantly see an increase in your credit score when you pay off your credit card debt due to the fact that 30% of your credit score is based upon your debt to credit ratio.

Also, FICO doesn't give as much weight to installment loans as compared to revolving debt. So, an installment loan that is the same amount as a revolving debt will carry less weight, meaning it will not lower your score as much. Lendingclub.com and Avant.com are 2 popular sites for getting small loans.

Dispute Letters

There are over 200 laws that are designed to protect your rights as a consumer. Your creditors commonly ignore these laws. They blatantly break the law, counting on you not knowing your rights well enough to challenge them. And the truth is, you would have to be an attorney to know and understand all the rights you actually have.

If you reviewed your credit reports and you don't agree with some of the information contained on your report, or even if any items are questionable, you can send a credit report dispute letter to each of the credit bureaus. The credit bureaus are obligated by law to investigate your dispute and they must either verify, correct, or delete the item from your record within 30 days.

Always include any copies of proof you may have such as, cancelled checks showing timely payments, paid off accounts, loans, and anything that will show the information is indeed erroneous.

The first dispute letter below is a great letter. You can alter the wording so that it is catered to your specific dispute. It is perfect for collections, inaccurate information, unverifiable, and unfair disputes.

Inaccurate, Unverifiable, Unfair, or Collection Letter

Date
Your Name
Your Address
Social Security Number
Re: Account Number

To Whom It My Concern:

This letter is regarding account xxxxxxxx, which you claim (insert a derogatory condition here, such as "I owe 7oo.oo" or "my account was charged off $900).

This formal notice that your claim is disputed.

Be advised that this is not a refusal to pay, but a notice sent pursuant to the Fair Debt Collection Practices Act, 15 USC 1692g Sec. 809 (b) that your claim is disputed and validation is requested. This is NOT a request for "verification" or proof of my mailing address, but a request for "VALIDATION" made pursuant to the above named Title and Section from the Fair Debt Collection Practices Act and the Fair Credit Reporting Act, along with the corresponding local state laws. I demand to see competent evidence bearing my signature, showing that I have or ever had, some contractual obligation to pay you.

Please also be aware that any negative mark found on my credit reports including: Experian, Transunion, and Equifax, from your company or any company that you request for a debt that I don't owe is a violation of the FCRA and FDCPA; therefore, if you cannot validate the debt, you must request that all credit reporting agencies delete the entry.

Pending the outcome of my investigation of any

evidence that you submit, you are instructed to take no action that could be determinantal to any of my credit reports.

Failure to respond within 30 days of receipt of this certified letter may result in small claims legal action against your company. And would be seeking a minimum of $1,000 in damages per violation for:

- Defamation
- Negligent Enablement of Identify Fraud
- Violation of the Fair Debt Collection Practices Act (incl8ding but not limited to Section 807-8)
- Violation of the Fair Credit Reporting Act (including but not limited to Section 623-b)

Please Note: This is a request for information only, and is not a statement, election, or waiver of status.

My contact information is as follows:
Your name (printed not signed)

Follow Up Letter For Account Reported Back Verified As "Accurate" From Above Letter

Date

Your Name

Your Address

Re: Account Number

Social Security Number

To Whom It May Concern:

This Letter is in response to your recent claim regarding account #xxx-xxx-xxx-xxx, which you claim (insert a derogatory condition here, such as "I owe $400" or "my account was charged off $900").

Yet again, you have failed to provide me with a copy of any viable evidence, bearing my signature, showing the account is being reported accurately.

Be advised that the description of the procedure used to determine the accuracy and completeness of the information is hereby requested.

Additionally, please provide the name, address, and telephone number of each person who personally verified this alleged account, so that I can inquire about how they "verified' without providing any proof, bearing m signature.

As per FTC opinion letter from Attorney John F. LeFevre, you should be aware that a printout of a bill or itemized document does not constituted verification.

Again, this is NOT a request for "verification" or proof of my mailing address, but a request for VALIDATION made pursuant to the above named Title and Section. I respectfully request that your offices provide me with competent evidence that I have any legal obligation to pay you. Please provide me with the following:

• A copy of any documents, veering my signature, showing that I have a legally binding contractual obligation to pay you the alluded amount
• Explain and show me how you calculated what you

say I owe;

• Provide me with copies of any papers that show I agreed to pay what you say I owe;

• Provide a verification or copy of any judgment if applicable;

• Identify the original creditor;

• Prove the Statute of Limitations has not expired on this account

• Show me that you are licensed to collect in my state

• Provide me with your license numbers and Registered Agent

At this time I will also inform you that if your offices have reported invalidated information to any of the 3 major Credit Bureau's (Equifax, Experian or TransUnion) this action might constitute fraud under both Federal and State Laws. Due to this fact, if any negative mark is found on any of my credit reports by your company or the company that you represent I will not hesitate in bringing legal action against you for the following:

• Violation of the Fair Credit Reporting Act
• Violation of the Fair Debt Collection Practices Act

• Defamation of Character

If your offices are able to provide the proper documentation as requested in the following Declaration, I will require at least 30 days to investigate this information and during such time all collection activity must cease and desist. Also during this validation period, if any action is taken which could be considered detrimental to any of my credit reports, I will consult with my legal counsel for suit. This includes any listing any information to a credit reporting repository that could be inaccurate or invalidated or verifying an account as accurate when in fact there is not provided proof that it is.

If your offices fail to respond to this validation request within 30 days from the date of your receipt, all references to this account must be deleted and completely removed from my credit file and a copy of such deletion request shall be sent to me immediately. I would also like to request, in writing, that no telephone contact be made by your offices to my home or to my place of employment.

If your offices attempt telephone communication with me, including but not limited to computer generated calls and calls or correspondence sent to or with any third parties, it will be considered harassment and I will have no choice but to file suit. All future communications with me MUST be done in writing and sent to the address noted in this letter by USPS.

It would be advisable that you assure that your records are in order before I am forced to take legal action. This is an attempt to correct your records, any information obtained shall be used for that purpose.

Best Regards,
Your Name (Printed First and Last)

P.S. Be aware that I am making a final goodwill attempt to have you clear up this matter. The listed item is accurate and incomplete and represents a very serious error in your reporting.

I am maintaining a careful record of my communications with you for the purpose of filing a complaint with the consumer Financial Protection

Bureau and the Attorney General's office, should you continue in the non-compliance of federal laws under the Fair Debt Collection Practices Act, the Fair Credit Reporting Act, and the corresponding local state laws. I further remind you that you may be liable for your willful non-compliance.

Inquiry Removal Letter

If you have recently acquired copies of your credit reports, you may notice an "Inquires" section toward the end of each of the reports. These credit inquires will be broken into two types – soft inquires and hard inquiries. You will want to have any unauthorized hard inquires removed from your credit reports as these may be affecting your credit score. A hard pull stays on your credit report for 2 years. And when initially done, it will drop your credit score approximately 5 points. Examples of hard pulls are; home loans, credit cards, car loans, most lenders will do hard pulls. Soft pulls do not harm your credit.

The Fair Credit Reporting Act allows only authorized inquiries to appear on your credit report. In order to remove a credit inquiry, you must challenge, generally the creditor or collection directly, whether the inquiring creditor had proper authorization to pull your credit file.

Date

Your Name

Your Address

Re: Account Number

Social Security Number

To Whom It May Concern:

I recently received a copy of my (insert name of bureau) credit report and I notice there is an unauthorized credit inquiry made by (insert name of creditor). I do not recall authorizing this credit inquiry and I understand you shouldn't be allowed to put an inquiry on my file unless I have authorized it. I am requesting you initiate an investigation into (insert name of creditor) inquiry to determine who requested this credit inquiry.

If you find I was not the one who authorized this inquiry, I ask that it be removed immediately from my credit file. Please be so kind as to forward me documentation that you have had the unauthorized inquiry removed.

If you find that I am in error, then please send me proof of this.

Thank you in advance,

Printed First and Last Name

Debt settlement is the process by which you are trying to come to an agreement with a collection agency regarding the amount of debt you owe. You want to negotiate a settlement so that you end up paying less than you owe. You can use this sample letter to send it to a collection agency confirming an offer to settle a debt and the amount the debt was settled for. It is very important this type of settlement is in writing and signed by all parties involved.

Debt Validation Letter — Request Collection Agency to Validate

Date:

Your Name

Your Address

Social Security Number

Re: Collection Account #

To Whom It May Concern,

I am sending this letter to you in response to a collection notice I received from you on (*date of letter)*. Be advised, this is not a refusal to pay, but validation is requested. I respectfully request that your office provide me with competent evidence that I have any legal obligation to pay you.

Please provide me with the following:

- Provide a statement which matches the balance being claimed
- Provide a list of charges that total the amount claim in your original letter
- Identify the original creditor

If your offices have reported inaccurate information to any of the three major Credit Bureau's (Equifax, Experian or TransUnion), said action might constitute fraud. Due to this fact, if any negative mark is found on any of my credit reports by your company or the company that you represent I will not hesitate in bringing legal action against you.

I would also like to request, in writing, that no

telephone contact be made by your offices to my home or to my place of employment. If your offices attempt telephone communication with me, including but not limited to computer generated calls or correspondence sent to any third parties, it will be considered harassment and I will have no choice but to file suit. All future communications with me MUST be done in writing and sent to the address noted in this letter.

Regards,

Printed First and Last Name

Debt Validation Letter (2)

Date:

Your Name

Your Address

Social Security Number

Re: Account Number

To whom it may concern,

This letter is being sent to you to inquire into the validity of a debt you are reporting on my credit report. Be advised that this is not a refusal to pay, but a notice sent pursuant to the Fair Debt Collection Practices Act, 15 USC 1692g Sec. 809 (b) that your claim is disputed, and validation is requested.

This is NOT a request for "verification" or proof of my mailing address, but a request for VALIDATION made pursuant to the above named Title and Section. I respectfully request that your offices provide me with competent evidence that I have any legal obligation to pay you.

Please provide me with the following:

- What the money you say I owe is for
- Explain and show me how you calculated what you say I owe
- Provide me with copies of any papers that show I agreed to pay what you say I owe
- Provide a verification or copy of any judgment if applicable
- Identify the original creditor
- Prove the Statue of Limitations has not expired on this account
- Show me that you are licensed to collect in my state
- Provide me with your license numbers and Registered Agent

At this time, I will inform you that if your offices have reported invalidated information to any of the 3 major Credit bureau's (Experian, Equifax, or TransUnion) this action might constitute fraud under both Federal and State Laws.

Due to this fact, if any negative mark is found on any of my credit reports by your company or the company that you represent I will not hesitate in bringing legal action against you for the following:

- Violation of the Fair Credit Reporting Act
- Violation of the Fair Debt Collection Practices Act
- Defamation of Character

If your offices are able to provide the proper documentation as requested in the following Declaration, I will require at least 30 days to investigate this information and during such time all collection activity must cease and desist.

Also during this validation period, if any action is taken which would be considered detrimental to any of my credit reports, I will consult with my legal counsel for suit. This includes any listing, any information to a credit reporting agency that could be inaccurate or invalidated or verifying an account as accurate when in fact there is no provided proof that is.

If your offices fail to respond to this validation request within 30 days from the date of your receipt, all references to this account must be deleted and completely removed from my credit file and a copy of such deletion request shall be sent to me immediately.

It would be advisable that you assure that your records are in order before I am forced to take legal action. This is an attempt to correct your records; any information obtained shall be used for that purpose.

Thank you in advance for your time,
Sincerely,
Printed First and Last Name

Pay For Deletion Letter

Date

Your Name

Your Address

Re: Account Number

Social Security Number

To whom it may concern:

In reference to the above listed account, I am writing this letter to offer you the opportunity to settle the alleged amount due to our mutual benefit. Please note that I do not acknowledge any liability for this debt in any form and I retain my right to request a full and complete debt verification and validation from your company.

However, I am willing to pay off a portion of this account as a show of goodwill under the following conditions:

- Your company will delete all references to this account from my credit profile at the 3 credit bureaus (Experian, TransUnion, and Equifax).
- You will not list this debt as a "settled account."
- Your company will accept this payment to satisfy the debt in full.
- Your company will not attempt to sell or transfer this debt to another creditor.
- You will make no mention of this agreement to outside third parties.

If you agree to these terms I will:

• Pay the amount of $XXX.XX via money order or certified cashier's check (aim for around 40% to 50% of the debt for newer accounts, and 30% to 40% of the debt for older accounts.)

Please understand that this is not a renewed promise to pay. This is a restricted settlement offer and you must agree to the terms above in order for payment to be made. I require your written agreement to these terms on company letterhead and signed by a representative who is authorized to enter into such agreements.

The terms of this offer will expire after 30 days. I look forward to your prompt and positive response.

Sincerely,

Printed First and Last Name

General Dispute Letter

Date:

Your Name

Your Address

Social Security Number

Re: Account Number and Name

To Whom It May Concern,

This letter is a formal request to correct inaccurate information contained in my credit file. The item(s) listed below is/are completely (insert appropriate words; incomplete misleading, incorrect, erroneous, outdated, etc.). I have listed the items below which are incorrect and need to be deleted from my credit file.

Line Item: (insert name of creditor, account number or line item number)

Item Description: (this info is found on your credit report)

In accordance with the federal Fair Credit Reporting Act I respectfully requires you to investigate my claim and if after your investigations you find my claim to be valid and accurate, I request that you immediately delete the item.

Furthermore, I request that you supply a corrected copy of my credit profile to me and all creditors who have received a copy within the last 6 months, or the last 2 years for employment purposes. Additionally, please provide me with the name, address, and telephone number of each credit grantor or other subscriber that you provided a copy of my credit report to within the past six months.

If your investigation shows the information to be accurate, I respectfully request that you forward to me a description of the procedure used to determine th accuracy and completeness of the item in question within 15 days of the completion of your re-investigation s required by the Fair Credit Reporting

Act.

I thank you for your consideration and cooperation. If you have any questions concerning this matter I can be reached at (insert your contact number here).

Sincerely,

Printed First and Last Name

Incorrect Balance Letter

Date:

Your Name

Your Address

Social Security Number:

Re: Account Number

I am contacting you because I have found some information that is inaccurate on my credit report.

The balance you are reporting I owe is incorrect and doesn't match my records. I request that you verify the information and remove any inaccurate information from my credit report as quickly as possible. The items in question are:

Insert: Creditors Name and Account Number

After doing so please provide me with an updated credit report reflecting the changes.

Thank you in advance for your time.

Printed First and Last Name.

Repo Letter

Date

Your Name

Your Address

Your Social Security Number

Collection Agency Name and Address

Car Dealer and Address

Re: Vin#

To whom it may concern,

This letter is a formal statement notifying the above parties that the accounts under VIN# (XXXXXXXX) are disputed.

The vehicle in question was purchased on or about (insert date), financed by (insert company), repossessed in the state of (insert state), and sold by (insert company/creditor) on or about (insert date).

Under the laws UCC 9.506 as well as State RISA and MVISA statutes, a deficiency can not be claimed unless all of the required notices were properly and timely given, and all of the allowable redemption and cure time limits were adhered to.

I demand proof that the repossession of the subject vehicle was legal in accordance with the following UCC:

- 9-506. EFFECT OF ERRORS OR OMISSIONS
- 9-611. NOTIFICATION BEFORE DISPOSITION OF COLLATERAL
- 9-612. TIMELINESS OF NOTIFICATIION BEFORE DISPOSTION OF COLLATERAL.
- 9-613. CONTENTS AND FORM OF NITIFICATIOIN BEFORE DISPOSTITION OF COLLATERAL.

You are required to provide me with copies of legal notices and proof of commercially reasonable manner of the notification and resale of subject vehicle.

If no such proof is provided within 15 days from receipt of this certified mail notice, the alleged claim of deficiency will be considered null and void, and any continued collection activities, or continued reporting of this invalid claim on my credit reports will be considered a violation of the FDCPA and FCRA.

In addition, if you singularly or severally fail to comply with the above requests, I reserve the right to seek damages against all parties, under all available State and Federal statues and including but not limited to UCC 9-625 remedies.

Furthermore, you are hereby notified that at no point in time and under no circumstances is your company; an employee of your company; a representative for your company or affiliates are to contact me or any family members by any means other than the US mail system.

Printed First and Last Name

Cease and Desist Letter

Date:

Your Name

Your Address

Re: Your Account Number

To whom it may concern,

This will serve as your legal notice pursuant to the Fair Debt Collection Act, 15 U.S.C. 1692, to cease and desist all further communications with me in regard to the above referenced debt or debts.

I have decided that I do not want to work with your collection agency or any other collection agency under any circumstances. I will contact the original creditor directly in order to resolve this matter. By sending this letter it is my intention to stop all your calls and collection activity from this day forth.

I also reserve the right to file suit against you for any further violations of this law. Please give this very important matter the utmost attention.

Thank you in advance,

Printed First and Last Name

It is vital to know your rights if you are in debt and searching for a solution to repair your credit.

Child Support, Taxes, And The IRS

If you are obligated to pay child support, college tuitions, income tax, the IRS can take your money. This means each year that you miss payments are at default, the IRS can and will deduct your entire tax refund to repay the debt.

The IRS is obligated by law to contact you before deducting any fees from your tax refunds.

Paying something toward your bill is better than avoiding your obligations. Another point you want to keep in mind is that when creditors write off a debt you may be required to pay taxes on the bill. Once a creditor writes off a debt it is sent to the IRS for review and if they choose to do so, you will still pay on that bill at the end of the year. They consider it earned income.

So, the best bet is when you get the first letter in the mail asking you to pay your bill is to write the lender or creditor and explain your situation politely and ask for an extension on payments. The truth is most creditors that lend or extend you credit hope that you are a returning customer and only suffering temporarily.

If you can keep the creditors on your side this is your best solution for avoiding complications. Another suggestion is to send in minimal payments on current bills that are overdue. Your next bill will be steep, but if you keep sending minimal payments until you are caught up, and you will not be hit will late payments that negatively affect your credit.

Avoiding Bad Credit Decisions

If you research the marketplace before coming to a purchasing decision, you are well on your way to avoiding bad credit and credit repair hassles. You want to consider all applications, including credit cards, student loans, mortgages, and car loans carefully to avoid being overcharged.

Making the wise decision ahead of the game is the ultimate solution to maintaining good credit. Most people when purchasing a car are not aware of the options available to them. Many will walk through the door of the dealership, fill out the application, and accept the terms & conditions when offered to them.

But, those who are aware will not accept the first offer. Why? Because the finance manager is trying to make money on the backend. That is his job. And he will increase the percentage rate you were given by the loan institution a couple of points. So, if you are unhappy with the terms, rates, or payments, take his final offer and go to the credit union and see if they can beat it. Credit unions are, in my professional opinion, the best place to get loans from. Unless you are getting a special promotional offer of 0%.

If you ever heard the many reports that swept the

pages of newspapers, television and the internet an unprecedented amount of families and individuals are filing bankruptcy. Bankruptcies are not only due to reckless spending, but also by financial hardships.

60% of the bankruptcies are by those families and individuals who make less than $30,000 a year and simply can't afford to deal with unexpected major expenses. And in 2016 alone there were almost 800,000 bankruptcies filed. This is because these people did not take the time to check the marketplace first and searching the options available to them. As you can see, the millions reported are in debt and searching for a way to repair their credit.

The solution then to avoiding bad credit and repair is to research, invest wisely, make good decisions, and budget. Being informed and educated is two of the best tools offered to us.

Top 9 Q & As

Q1. What Interest Rate Are They Offering And Why Should I Care?

Answer: The interest rate on your credit account plays a serious role in your ability to keep up with your payments. If possible, make payment in full. Keep in mind that making full payment may not always be possible. This is why you need to consider carefully the interest rate that you are agreeing to.

The interest rate will apply on all minimum payments. An example is below:

Balance owed on account   : $350.00
Interest Rate   : 5.7% (.057)
Minimum Payment   : $19.95

Think about this, $19.95 only pays for the interest that is going to be added to the balance owed. You may think that you can subtract $19.95 from the $350.00 owed, however, do not forget to add the .057 to the balance. At this rate, your balance owed will go down very slowly and continue to accumulate interest on a monthly basis.

Q2. Should I Make Payments On Time?

Answer: While this answer seems obvious, let's look at a little further. Do not make payments before 30 days of the due date and do not make a payment after 15 days after due date. Payments received after 15 days, with most companies, are considered late, some companies do not even have a grace period, and payments made before 30 days are not going to build your credit. The bureaus want to see a payment history and if you pay the bill before the bill is due, then there will be no bill. Make sense?

The most effective way to pay and build your credit is to pay 90% of the bill when the bill is due, and then pay the remaining 10% five days to seven days after. It is an extra step, but will even increase your credit score more quickly due to the algorithm the credit card companies use to determine your score.

Q3. Can I Apply For Credit Numerous Times A Year?

Answer: If you do, you can easily be denied credit because those actions are perceived as shopping for credit. If you are suspected of shopping for credit, your creditors will deny you. You can keep track of how many times you have applied for credit and with who by looking at your credit report. Your credit report shows all the people have inquired into your report for the last 2 years. After 2 years, the listing drops off your report. Once you begin paying a creditor, take it slow. You are going to get many offers for credit and it is extremely tempting to take them all up on their offers.

Q4. Should I Keep All My Receipts And Contracts?

Answer: Keep all of your receipts for payments made to any creditor. Yes, creditors have been known to misplace a payment received, let's hope it isn't yours. Rest assured if it is, providing you kept your receipts.

Saving your contract with any creditor is highly advised. In the event that a dispute should arise, the creditor will be sure to throw in comments concerning your agreement and signature on the contract.

Q5. Can I Dispute My Credit Report Over The Phone?

Answer: Yes, you can do your disputes over the phone, but again, it's not a wise decision. It's almost as bad as disputing online because there is no paper trail to confirm your actions.

If you want the best chance of getting negative items removed from your credit report, write a letter and keep careful records of all communications you send and receive from both creditors and the credit bureaus.

Q6. What Items Can I Dispute On My Credit Report?

Answer: Anything that is reported on your credit report can be disputed including personal information, credit inquiries, charge offs, collections, bankruptcies, foreclosures, repossessions, tax liens, judgments, etc.

Be very careful that you don't dispute positive items on your credit report. Once they are removed, it's pretty much impossible to get them back on your credit report.

Q7. What Is The Process For Disputing?

Answer: The process for disputing:

1. Get a copy of your credit reports.
2. Look for inaccurate, incomplete, unverifiable, questionable, and obsolete information.
3. Write dispute letters.
4. Make and keep copies and dates of letters.
5. Send disputes letters to CRAs and/or creditors.

6. If the info is "verified" as correct, then send follow up letters and continue to dispute.

7. If items inaccurate items do not come off of credit reports, file a lawsuit.

Q8. What Is The Difference Between Good Credit and Bad Credit On Loans?

Credit Card With $7,000 Debt:

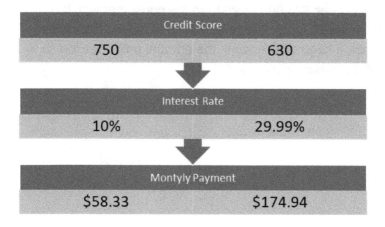

Credit Score	
750	630

Interest Rate	
10%	29.99%

Montyly Payment	
$58.33	$174.94

Over the lifetime of the loan the consumer with the 750 credit score will pay $20,998.80 while the consumer with the 630 credit score will pay $62,978.40. That is a huge difference. The lower credit score consumer will pay almost $42,000 dollars more than the better credit score consumer.

Insurance

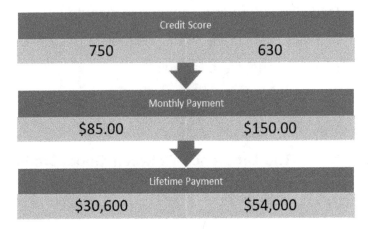

The consumer with the lower credit score will end up paying over $23,000 more than the consumer with the better credit score, over the lifetime of having insurance. Again, a huge difference in the amount paid over the lifetime of having insurance.

Mortgage $350,000

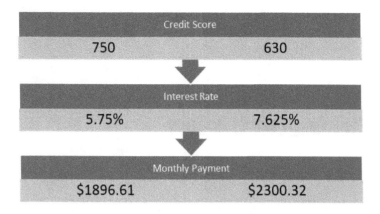

The consumer with the lower credit score will end up paying $145,335.60 more than the consumer with the better credit score over the lifetime of the loan. Imagine what you could do with $145.335.60.

Best Strategies For Building Credit

You are about to learn some of the best tactics and strategies for building credit that I have learned over the past 20 years in the sales business. Building your credit is important in today's time and economy, especially since the laws are changing. We are moving into a system that is making it difficult for us to get ahead unless we have excellent, or at most good credit history. Credit is important to rent, obtain student loans, and apply for loans or credit cards, as well as getting jobs. Building credit is essential for your future survival.

Building Credit History

If you do not have any credit at all, you will need to start somewhere. One strategy for building credit is to apply for a credit card or a personal loan and ask your family members or friends to co-sign the application. Once you have opened an account, make sure you meet all monthly obligations, since if you miss any payments at all your co-signer is responsible. If you do not have a credit history, you might want to opt for credit cards issued by gas stations, or else open an account with a department store.

These cards are relatively easy to get hold of, and it helps you to build credit. After you established some line of credit, make your payments faithfully and after about six months you will be entitled to more credit. Never take out more than you need when applying for a loan and always check the interest rates and upfront fees to avoid overpaying.

If you have someone to co-sign, make sure that family member or friend has established credit and their history is not delinquent. Once you get the card or loan, make sure you meet each month's installments. If you miss any payments the co-signers are responsible to pick up the tab. do not make enemies, pay your dues on time. After about six months of using your credit card or else paying on the loan you will have notoriety and able to apply for credit cards or loans in your own name.

Becoming An Authorized User

One of the quickest and easiest ways to establish credit, when you have no credit, is becoming an Authorized User on someone else's credit card. If you have a friend or family member with good, or better yet excellent credit, then you can take advantage of it by "piggybacking" off of their good credit. What this means is you will benefit from their longstanding good credit history.

When you become an Authorized User, your friend or family member with established credit, signs and allows you permission to become a user of their card and account. This is a noble thing to do for someone. This will allow you the benefits of making purchases on the person's card but not liable for the payments. Do not misuse the good deed being offered to you. Do not use the card unless you are given permission to.

"Piggybacking" has 2 major benefits for you. First it will give you a length of credit history, which is 15% of your credit score and second, it will allow you to receive the good standing payment history, which is 35% of your credit score.

Authorized User accounts are so effective for boosting credit scores that many companies actually sell them as "seasoned tradelines." And buying a "seasoned tradeline" for the purposes of qualifying for a home loan is fraud.

3 Ways Significantly Increase Your Credit Score Within 30 Days

Become an Authorized User - One of the best ways to increase your credit score within 30 days is becoming an Authorized User, which we just discussed. It is so effective that it has increased one's credit score hundreds of points in a month's time.

Apply For New Line Of Credit - The second credit secret for increasing your credit score within 30 days is getting approved for new credit. If you apply and get approved for a new line of credit, say with a credit card with a credit limit of $5,000 and you already have $5,000 on another credit card with $3,000 debt on it. You just went from 60% credit card utilization to 30% credit card utilization which will have a positive effect on your credit score. 30% of your credit scores is based upon your debt to credit ratio.

Increase Your Credit Limit – Again, your debt to

credit ratio is 30% of your credit score. If you call and request a credit limit increase with your credit card companies, then it will automatically drop your debt to credit ratio which in turn will increase your credit score. These small powerful secrets were and are being used every day to significantly increase credit scores within 30 days.

Join A Credit Union

Credit Unions are one of the best institutions you can be a part of for building and/or maintaining good credit. Credit Unions tend to have lower interest rates on loans and credit cards, which is exactly what you want with loans and credit cards and they are more lenient in granting them.

One of the best credit unions to join is the Navy Federal Credit Union. They have fantastic rates on loans and credit cards, and free checking and savings accounts.

They've also been known to give high limit unsecured

credit cards to people with bad credit.

Navy Federal primarily serves members with military affiliations meaning someone in your immediate family has to have served in the military.

Keep All Your Records

Letters are probably better than phoning creditors, or online disputing since some creditors could care less about your situation and may threaten you. Another good reason for writing letters is that (copy in writing) is more valuable in a courtroom than a conversation on the phone. If something is said or an agreement is reached, and the creditor later denies his or her claims then you can present this to any courtroom and they will listen to you first.

Any documents that pertain to your credit history should be stored in a safe area. If you send letters to your creditors keep a copy of each letter sent and store it in a safe area. If you have credit cards and used the card to purchase an item or use a service and this person sold you a defected item or else provided bad service, you DO NOT have to make payment toward the charges.

You do however, have to dispute the charges with the services or stores that sold you the product or service. If the sources refuse to give you a useable item, or else reimburse you for a service or product you have the right to deny payment.

Once you have disputed the charges with the sources you will then contact your card provider and let them know what occurred.

Collection Agencies

Collection agencies are not as kind as the lenders so, therefore be warned...the collection agencies are on the loose.

We must understand how collection agencies work in order to find a way to stop hassling phone calls and letters. Collection agencies are a third-party source hired by creditors after the creditor has made every attempt to collect a debt without success. Collection agencies will search high and low and often play nasty little tricks trying to hunt you down.

If you changed your address and typed your credit card into an online database, do not be surprise when the debt you tried to outrun catches up with you. Collection agencies tap into all types of resources in an effort to hunt down debtors. Collection personnel searches through phone directories, databases online, makes phone calls posing as a friend to luring the debtor in, sifts through the records at the post office, and so on.

There is no stone unturned when it comes to collection agencies in a search to find a debtor. The upside is many of the collection agencies make mistakes by hiring low waged servants to handle the job of finding debtors. When they are sifting through the files, they often loose contact since they have millions of records each day. It may take up to 6 months to feel like you are making any progress at all on your credit with your payment arrangements, but rest assured that your credit will fall into place within a year. Remember, it didn't take a day to ruin your credit, and it will not take a day to correct it.

The Top 7 Creditor/Collection Agency Violations

As a consumer, it is important that you are aware of your rights with debt collectors. Debt collectors have specific rules they must follow when they are collecting a debt from you according to the Fair Debt Collection Practices Act. The FDCPA has strict guidelines about what the debt collectors can and cannot do.

Here are the top 7 violations of these guidelines:

1. Call you before 8am or after 9pm
2. Give false credit information to a credit reporting company
3. Lie about the amount you owe

4. Contact a third party such as an employer or friend for any reason other than getting contact information
5. Threaten to garnish or sell your property
6. Continue to contact you after a written letter has been sent asking them to stop calling you
7. Must inform you that they are a debt collector attempting to collect a debt

What To Do If A Debt Collector Violates The FDCPA

According to LaToya Irby in her work on, Reporting Debt Collectors Who Violate The FDCPA:

"There are several things to do if a debt collector violated your rights, for example by calling you even after you sent a cease and desist letter.

You have the right to take these actions against a debt collector that violates the FDCPA.

File a complaint with the Consumer Financial Protection Bureau against the collector. The CFPB can investigate your complaint and other complaints against that collector and penalize them for breaking the law. In some cases, consumers may be entitled to a partial refund of fees paid to a debt collector who has violated the FDPCA.

File a complaint with your state's attorney general. Like the CFPB, your state attorney general can take legal action against a debt collector who violates the law.

You can also file a complaint with the Better Business Bureau. While the Better Business Bureau (BBB) cannot take legal action against debt collectors who violate the FDCPA. They can help mediate disputes against debt collectors. The BBB also reports consumer complaints against businesses and can help warn other consumer about problems with particular debt collectors. File a civil suit in your state or federal court for up to $1,000 including damages. The FDCPA gives you the right to sue a debt collector who has violated your rights. Consult with a consumer rights attorney to discuss your case.

When you file a complaint or suit against a debt collector, have as much evidence supporting your claim as possible, including dates and times of phone calls, name of the collection agency, name of the person you spoke with, and specific details about the violation."

Defaults

Defaults are non-payments on accounts that are sent in to collections. When a person is in default, they are subjected to lawsuits, liens, judgments, and other complicated situations. If you are a student struggling to pay student loans, a renter struggling to meet monthly bills, or a homeowner battling to stay out of debt you might want to know what is available to you.

If you have a college loan, which means you have a loan from the government you can ask for a default, which gives, you time to repay the loan. Other types of defaults include insurance policies, bills, car loans, personal loans, and other types of credit lines.

Sometimes we are subject to debts that may not be ours. There are thousands of collection agencies and credit reporting services throughout the US. Sometimes there are errors sent to the credit bureaus that put the default on your credit file. Once the default goes on your credit file it remains there until the bill is paid in full or disputed and removed completely. Now, if you did not make the purchase the first thing you want to do is file a dispute.

The major problem however, defaults remain on your credit file for a period of time before they are removed. The upside is the ability to fight for your rights and dispute the allegations made against you. It will take some time and effort on your part, but it can be done.

After you have disputed the issues with the providers, you will next contact your credit card lender and inform them of the defaults on your credit report. DO NOT pay on items or services that are in dispute, since this means the creditors will view you in a different light. And, normally, the credit card companies will send you a letter or email telling you not to pay anything until the dispute is resolved. If it is with someone like your insurance company, then ask the agent what you should do. Because you do not want to have your policy lapse and cost you more money.

If your insurance policies are delinquent, you might lose your coverage, which in most cases, might be more trouble than you realize. Read all terms & agreements as well as any other fine prints before obligating yourself to a contract. If there is a default against you on your policy, contact your provider immediately and try to work out a plan.

By making contact, you could save your insurance as well as additional debts added to your accounts. Anyone that lends you a line of creditor subjects you to defaults if you cannot make payments. If you have defaults on your credit report, make sure that you work to pay the debts down to avoid complications and your credit score falling even further. Proactive vs. Reactive is the key here. If you know you will be unable to make the payments, call the creditor and inform them of your situation. And, send them some amount of payment. Some payment is better than no payment.

Identity Theft Victims And LifeLock

Identity theft happens every 2 seconds in the United States and it can happen to anyone. In fact, A major credit bureau recently reported a breach potentially impacting 143 million people. 143 million!! Now, that is scary.

Identity theft victims have done absolutely nothing wrong, yet lose simply because someone has stolen their identity and run up their bills. You see, the Internet is swarming with predators just waiting to mess up someone else's life. Instead of these "people", if you want to call them people, getting a legitimate job and having a real life they would rather destroy someone else's.

There are several ways that your Identity can be stolen and these people that do it do not care who they hurt or how severely. Some of these people may stand over your shoulder peeking down at you while you are keying in your PIN number at the bank or in line at the grocery store. You might have even been in a relationship and the person decides he/she owns you and when you break up that person takes your identity. Or, there is a breach in one of the credit agencies or a major retailer and your identity is stolen. It happens every single day.

If you are a victim of Identity Theft then you are well-aware of how difficult it can be to get back on your feet again. Identity Theft victims often have to go through an exhausting series of steps to repair their credit and identity.

With the number of hackers growing each year and the number of identities stolen steadily increasing each year, I 100% believe that everyone should have LifeLock for themselves. You can get it for next to nothing. Just go to updatecreditrepair.com and click on products. LifeLock is just one of the products my company offers. LifeLock will "Lock" in your social security number so no one can run it for credit, or to purchase anything. You will be the only one with access to "unlock" it and have your credit ran.

So, is there a solution for Identity Theft victims and how can they repair the credit? Yes. First, it is important to avoid Identity Theft by protecting your Social Security Card, Driver License and other important information about yourself.

The solution is then protecting your identity with shields that no one can break through. If you are a victim of Identity Theft, then your identity needs to be protected now more so than ever. This may sound crazy, but since your information stolen and used once, they can do it again. So, you will need to stay alert to the activities that affect your credit report. It is important that you keep updated copies of your reports at all time. If you notice activity, immediately dispute the claims against you.

Be sure to file a police report since you will need these reports to show the 3 bureaus and others that your identity has been stolen. Once you receive the reports make sure you send copies to each credit bureau so that the companies can get you on record.

The companies are going to put up a Freud Alert once the copies are evaluated.

You will also need to report any checks that you suspect were stolen. Monitor your banking account at all times to make sure that no out of place activities are going on. It is important that you alert your utility providers and anyone that you have open accounts with. If you have credit cards report them immediately to get replacements. You may even want to cancel your current bank account and open a new account.

This will offer a source of protection. It is also important that you contact your Social Security Office to find out if your Social Security Number has been used out of place. If actions have been listed on your card, be sure to let the Social Security Administrators know.

Finally, you will need to contact Washington D.C. or the Identity Theft Clearinghouse, Federal Trade Commissions and let them know you are a victim of Identity Theft.

Once you have made contact with the 3 credit bureaus, Equifax, Transunion, and Experian, the bureaus will reach out to you with what you will need to do next. Again, I highly recommend everyone having a fraud alert/identity protection in place for their social security number and personal information.

Once You Have Established Good Credit

The most important thing to do with regard to your credit is take pride, protect, respect and especially enjoy it. Having good credit is a luxury and can widen the horizons of possibilities for you and your future.

Once you've established some credit, take caution with accepting credit offers from other creditors, look into the interest rate the lenders are offering, consider the monthly obligation in addition to your other financial responsibilities such as rent, utility bills, car insurance, groceries, laundry expenses, gas, day care, etc., and feel free to decline credit offers.

In the beginning of your adventure with new credit accounts, it can be very exciting to have several creditors offering advances, it can be an uplifting and powerful event, however, pursue with caution in order to maintain a healthy credit rating and score. Keep your credit history in mind and respect the great task that you have accomplished by establishing credit with caution.

Credit Repair Laws

Fair Debt Collections Practices Act - There are certain laws issued for people that have bad credit and to know these laws is important to protect all those involved in your life. The Federal Legislation and several other agencies including the Fair Credit Reporting Act (FCRA) to protect you from collection agencies and creditors. If you have bad credit you really want to read this article especially if you are being harassed by creditors or else threatened. First, we are going to look at what steps debtors can take to protect their status.

According to the FDCPA, which is a law in place to protect consumers from unfair practices of collection agencies that dictates what they can and cannot while collecting a debt from you, debtors have the right to ask collection agencies or any source hassling them for debt collection to stop hassling them. You must contact the collection agencies immediately and request that they stop communication with your completely. It is important to word your letter wisely avoiding giving them ammunition against you. You can do this if your collection agency has claimed a lawsuit against you, or if the date has ended, where the creditors can no longer contact you.

If the collection agency has written several letters or made several phone calls threatening you with a lawsuit, you can write an informal letter asking the agencies to stop nagging you. If you have a current debt, it is wise to negotiate with the creditors, since some may reduce your balance or even drop the debt completely. If the debt is older than seven years, it is important that you DO NOT communicate with a collection agency regarding the bill. At the seven-year period, the account should have been removed from your credit report. If it has not these people are in violation of the law.

Collection agencies under the law cannot correspond with you by sending mail to your address with symbols or labels. Collection agencies cannot call your mom and dad, or any family member regarding your debt. The collection agencies are obligated by law to cease communication if you have been subpoenaed to court.

Collection agencies are prohibited from impersonating law enforcement or government officials in an effort to collect a debt. At no time is a collection agency allowed to make available to the public information regarding your debts. Collection agencies are prohibited from sending letters, making phones calls, or acting out any form of communication that insinuates false impersonation.

It is also against the law for collection agencies to repeatedly call your home requesting you or threatening you to pay the debt. If a collection agency phones your home, they must comply by the law and identify their name and the companies name within one minute of the phone conversation. Finally, collection agencies are prohibited to list debtors on the 'deadbeat' list. Many laws and regulations apply to both collection agencies and debtors. Therefore, when you know the law you have strength to protect yourself and a possible solution to avoid the law.

Fair Credit Reporting Act – The FCRA is a U.S. legislation put in place to promote the accuracy, fairness, and privacy of consumers information contained in the files of the CRAs. This is one of the most powerful reasons we as consumers have the ability to dispute and remove inaccurate, incomplete, or suspicious items on our credit reports.

Fair Credit Billing Act - The FCBA was put in place as an amendment of the Truth in Lending Act with the purpose to protect consumers from unfair billing practices and to provide a system to address billing errors with the credit card companies. Billing errors include; charges for merchandise that wasn't received, unauthorized charges, unposted payments, etc.

Contact Information For The CRAs

Equifax

P.O. Box 7404256

Atlanta, GA 30374

Phone Number 1-888-202-4025

Experian

Dispute Department

P.O. Box 9701

Allen, TX 75013

Phone Number 1-888-397-3742

TransUnion

Consumer Solutions

P.O. Box 2000

Chester, PA 19022

Phone Number 1-855-681-3196

<u>Conclusion</u>

Finally, in order to start repairing your credit score, you must begin a chronological sequence of actions that will need credit reporting bureaus, creditors, debt collectors, and other entities with which you engage in financial transactions to guarantee that the information they collect, report, and /or sell about you is precise. This information is in use to count on your credit score and when it is inappropriate, incorrect, out-of-date, or something wrong on it may harm your credit rating instantly and as well as the credit score as years beyond its initial entry into your credit file.

Different view of repairing your credit score affects understanding credit and how several types of credit may help or damage your credit ranking and credit score. You need to evaluate your ability to capitalize on the different credit options and take advantage of those credit types that will be virtually advantageous to you at any given time or in any given condition. Life cases such as graduation, employment, or marriage may affect your ability to get or sustain certain types of credit. For your financial and credit histories, as accumulated and recorded by credit reporting bureau, may be responsible for improving or damaging your credit ranking and credit score if you are not responsible for monitoring the information that is compiled on you and take steps to make sure that it is correct.

While there are many factors involved in repairing your credit score, your personal commitment to repairing your score is important. You, not the credit reporting agencies, your creditors, nor the government is going to take responsibility to repair your credit score for you.

This book will give you all of the information that you'll need to begin repairing your credit score now.

Subscribe to our blog updatecreditrepair.com
And follow us on Facebook at Update Your Credit

CPSIA information can be obtained
at www.ICGtesting.com
Printed in the USA
FSHW012045240219
55916FS

9 780578 201061